Contents

Warm Blue Crab Bruschetta

   4 cups peeled, seeded and diced Roma or plum tomatoes
   1 cup diced white onion
   2 teaspoons minced garlic
   ⅓ cup olive oil
   2 tablespoons balsamic vinegar
   ½ teaspoon dried oregano
   2 tablespoons sugar
   1 pound lump blue crabmeat
1½ teaspoons Kosher salt
   ½ teaspoon cracked black pepper
   ⅓ cup minced fresh basil
   2 baguettes, sliced and toasted

1. Combine tomatoes, onion, garlic, oil, vinegar, oregano and sugar in **CROCK-POT®** slow cooker. Cover; cook on **LOW 2 hours.**

2. Pick out and discard any shell or cartilage from crabmeat. Add crabmeat, salt and pepper to **CROCK-POT®** slow cooker. Stir gently to mix, taking care not to break up crabmeat lumps. Cover; cook on **LOW 1 hour.**

3. Fold in basil. Serve on baguette slices.

makes 16 servings

Serving Suggestion: Crab topping can also be served with Melba toast or whole grain crackers.

Steamed Pork Buns

½ **container (18 ounces) refrigerated cooked shredded pork in barbecue sauce***

1 **tablespoon Asian garlic chili sauce**

1 **container (16.3 ounces) refrigerated biscuits (8 biscuits)**

Dipping Sauce (recipe follows)

Sliced green onions (optional)

*Look for pork in plain, not smoky, barbecue sauce. Substitute chicken in barbecue sauce, if desired.

1. Combine pork and chili sauce in medium bowl. Split biscuits in half. Roll or stretch each biscuit into 4-inch circle. Spoon 1 tablespoon pork onto center of each biscuit. Gather edges around filling and press to seal.

2. Generously butter 2-quart baking dish that fits inside **CROCK-POT®** slow cooker. Arrange filled biscuits in single layer, overlapping slightly if necessary. Cover dish with buttered foil, butter side down.

3. Place small rack in **CROCK-POT®** slow cooker or prop up baking dish with a few equal-size potatoes. Add 1 inch hot water (water should not come to top of rack). Place baking dish on rack. Cover; cook on **HIGH 2 hours.**

4. Meanwhile, prepare Dipping Sauce. Garnish pork buns with green onions, if desired. Serve with Dipping Sauce.

makes 8 servings

Dipping Sauce

Combine 2 tablespoons rice vinegar, 2 tablespoons soy sauce, 4 teaspoons sugar and 1 teaspoon toasted sesame oil in small bowl until sugar dissolves. Sprinkle with 1 tablespoon minced green onion just before serving.

Creamy Cheesy Spinach Dip

> 2 packages (10 ounces each) frozen chopped spinach, thawed
> 2 cups chopped onions
> 1 teaspoon salt
> ½ teaspoon garlic powder
> ¼ teaspoon black pepper
> 12 ounces pasteurized processed cheese spread with jalapeño peppers, cubed
>   Cherry tomatoes with pulp removed (optional)
>   Sliced cucumbers (optional)
>   Assorted crackers (optional)

1. Drain spinach and squeeze dry, reserving ¾ cup liquid. Place spinach, reserved liquid, onions, salt, garlic powder and pepper into 1½-quart or other small-sized **CROCK-POT®** slow cooker; stir to blend. Cover; cook on **HIGH 1½ hours.**

2. Stir in cheese spread. Cover; cook on **HIGH 30 minutes** or until cheese spread is melted. Fill cherry tomato shells, spread on cucumber slices or serve with crackers, as desired.

makes about 4 cups

Tip: To thaw spinach quickly, remove paper wrapper from spinach containers. Microwave on HIGH 3 to 4 minutes or until just thawed.

Chicken and Asiago Stuffed Mushrooms

- 20 large button mushrooms, stems removed and reserved
- 3 tablespoons extra virgin olive oil, divided
- ¼ cup finely chopped onion
- 2 cloves garlic, minced
- ¼ cup Madeira wine
- ½ pound uncooked chicken sausage, removed from casings or ground chicken
- 1 cup grated Asiago cheese
- ¼ cup Italian-style seasoned dry bread crumbs
- 3 tablespoons chopped fresh parsley
- ½ teaspoon salt
- ¼ teaspoon black pepper

1. Lightly brush mushroom caps with 1 tablespoon oil; set aside. Finely chop mushroom stems.

2. Heat remaining 2 tablespoons oil in large nonstick skillet over medium-high heat. Add onion; cook 1 minute or until just beginning to soften. Add mushroom stems; cook 5 to 6 minutes or until beginning to brown. Stir in garlic; continue cooking 1 minute.

3. Pour in wine; cook 1 minute. Add sausage; cook 3 to 4 minutes or until no longer pink, stirring to break up meat. Drain fat. Remove from heat; cool 5 minutes. Stir in cheese, bread crumbs, parsley, salt and pepper.

4. Divide mushroom-sausage mixture among mushroom caps, pressing slightly to compress. Place stuffed mushroom caps in single layer in **CROCK-POT®** slow cooker. Cover; cook on **LOW 4 hours** or on **HIGH 2 hours** or until mushrooms are tender and filling is heated through.

makes 4 to 5 servings

Sun-Dried Tomato Appetizer

3 cups chopped onion

3 jars (about 7 ounces each) oil-packed sun-dried tomatoes, drained and finely chopped

3 tablespoons sugar

1 tablespoon minced garlic

Grated 2-inch piece peeled fresh ginger

1 teaspoon herbes de Provence

½ teaspoon salt

½ cup red wine vinegar

1 package (8 ounces) cream cheese

Fresh basil sprigs, for garnish

Assorted crackers

1. Place onion, tomatoes, sugar, garlic, ginger, herbes de Provence and salt in 2-quart **CROCK-POT®** slow cooker. Pour in vinegar; stir gently to mix. Cover; cook on **LOW 4 to 5 hours** or on **HIGH 3 hours,** stirring occasionally. Let mixture cool before using.

2. To serve, slice cream cheese in half horizontally (use dental floss for clean cut) and separate pieces. Spread ⅓ cup tomato mixture onto 1 cream cheese half. Top with second cream cheese half and spread ⅓ cup tomato mixture on top. Garnish with fresh basil sprigs and serve with crackers. Refrigerate or freeze remaining tomato mixture for future use.

makes 8 servings

Tip: Tomato and cream cheese appetizer may be assembled in advance, wrapped and refrigerated until serving time.

Shrimp Fondue Dip

    1 pound shrimp, peeled, cleaned and deveined
    ½ cup water
    ½ teaspoon salt, divided
    2 tablespoons butter
    4 teaspoons Dijon mustard
    6 slices thick-sliced white bread, crusts removed*
    2 eggs, beaten
    1 cup milk
    ¼ teaspocn black pepper
    2 cups (8 ounces) shredded Gruyère or Swiss cheese
      Crusty French bread, sliced

Thick-sliced bread is often sold as "Texas toast" in supermarket bread aisles.

1. Coat **CROCK-POT®** slow cooker with nonstick cooking spray. Place shrimp, water and ¼ teaspoon salt in small saucepan. Cover; cook over medium heat about 3 minutes or until shrimp is pink and cooked through. Remove shrimp with slotted spoon; reserve ½ cup broth.

2. Combine butter and mustard in small bowl. Spread mixture onto bread slices. Cut bread into 1-inch cubes; set aside.

3. Beat eggs, milk, reserved broth, remaining ¼ teaspoon salt and pepper in small bowl; set aside.

4. Spread one third of bread cubes in bottom of **CROCK-POT®** slow cooker. Top with one third of shrimp. Sprinkle with one third of cheese. Repeat layers two more times. Pour egg mixture over layers. Use rubber spatula to push bread below surface to absorb liquid. Line lid with two paper towels. Cover tightly; cook on **LOW 2 hours** or until mixture is hot and thick. Serve on French bread.

makes 5 cups

Tip: For a party, use a **CROCK-POT®** slow cooker on the LOW or WARM setting to keep hot dips and fondues warm.

Maple-Glazed Meatballs

1½ cups ketchup

1 cup maple syrup or maple-flavored syrup

⅓ cup soy sauce

1 tablespoon quick-cooking tapioca

1½ teaspoons ground allspice

1 teaspoon dry mustard

2 packages (about 16 ounces each) frozen fully cooked meatballs, partially thawed and separated

1 can (20 ounces) pineapple chunks in juice, drained

1. Combine ketchup, maple syrup, soy sauce, tapioca, allspice and mustard in 4½-quart **CROCK-POT®** slow cooker.

2. Carefully stir meatballs and pineapple chunks into ketchup mixture.

3. Cover; cook on **LOW 5 to 6 hours.** Stir before serving. Serve warm; insert cocktail picks, if desired.

makes about 48 meatballs

Tip: For a quick main dish, serve meatballs over hot cooked rice.

Moroccan Spiced Chicken Wings

¼ cup orange juice

3 tablespoons tomato paste

2 teaspoons ground cumin

1 teaspoon curry powder

1 teaspoon ground turmeric

½ teaspoon ground cinnamon

½ teaspoon ground ginger

1 teaspoon salt

1 tablespoon olive oil

5 pounds chicken wings, tips removed and split at joints

1. Stir together orange juice, tomato paste, cumin, curry, turmeric, cinnamon, ginger and salt in large bowl; set aside.

2. Heat oil in large nonstick skillet over medium-high heat. Add wings and brown in several batches, about 6 minutes per batch. Transfer wings to bowl with sauce as they are cooked. When all wings are cooked, toss well to coat.

3. Place wings in 4½-quart **CROCK-POT®** slow cooker. Cover and cook on **LOW 6 to 7 hours** or on **HIGH 3 to 3½ hours** or until tender.

makes 8 servings

Spicy Sweet and Sour Cocktail Franks

2 packages (8 ounces each) cocktail franks

½ cup ketchup or chili sauce

½ cup apricot preserves

1 teaspoon hot pepper sauce

Additional hot pepper sauce (optional)

Combine all ingredients in 1½-quart **CROCK-POT®** slow cooker; mix well. Cover; cook on **LOW 2 to 3 hours.** Serve warm or at room temperature with additional hot pepper sauce, if desired.

makes about 4 dozen

MOROCCAN SPICED CHICKEN WINGS

Bagna Cauda

¾ **cup olive oil**

6 **tablespoons butter, softened**

12 **anchovy fillets, drained**

6 **cloves garlic, peeled**

⅛ **teaspoon red pepper flakes**

Assorted foods for dipping, such as endive spears, cauliflower floretes, cucumber spears, carrot sticks, zucchini spears, red bell pepper pieces, sugar snap peas or crusty Italian bread slices

Place olive oil, butter, anchovies, garlic and red pepper flakes in blender or food processor; process about 30 seconds or until smooth. Spoon mixture into **CROCK-POT®** slow cooker. Cover; cook on **LOW 2 hours** or on **HIGH 1 hour** or until mixture is heated through. Turn to **WARM** and serve with assorted dippers.

makes 10 to 12 servings

Tip: Bagna cauda is a warm Italian dip similar to the more famous fondue. The name is derived from "bagno caldo," meaning "warm bath" in Italian. This dip should be kept warm while serving, just like you would fondue.

Thai Coconut Chicken Meatballs

1 pound ground chicken

2 green onions, chopped

1 clove garlic, minced

2 teaspoons toasted sesame oil

2 teaspoons mirin (rice wine)

1 teaspoon fish sauce

1 tablespoon canola oil

½ cup unsweetened canned coconut milk

¼ cup chicken broth

1 teaspoon Thai red curry paste

2 teaspoons brown sugar

2 teaspoons lime juice

1 tablespoon cornstarch

2 tablespoons cold water

1. Combine chicken, green onions, garlic, sesame oil, mirin and fish sauce in large bowl. Mix well to combine and shape into meatballs about 1½ inches in diameter.

2. Heat canola oil in large skillet over medium-high heat. Add meatballs and cook, rolling to brown on all sides. Transfer to **CROCK-POT®** slow cooker. Add coconut milk, broth, curry paste and brown sugar. Cover; cook on **HIGH 3½ to 4 hours.** Stir in lime juice.

3. Stir cornstarch into cold water, mixing until smooth. Stir in additional water as needed to reach consistency of heavy cream. Stir into sauce in **CROCK-POT®** slow cooker. Cook, uncovered, on **HIGH 10 to 15 minutes** or until sauce is slightly thickened and evenly coats meatballs.

makes 4 to 5 servings

Tip: Meatballs that are of equal sizes will cook at the same rate and be done at the same time. To ensure your meatballs are the same size, pat seasoned ground meat into an even rectangle and then slice into even rows and columns. Roll each portion into a smooth ball.

Stuffed Baby Bell Peppers

1 tablespoon extra virgin olive oil

½ onion, chopped

½ pound ground beef, chicken or turkey

½ cup cooked white rice

3 tablespoons chopped fresh parsley

2 tablespoons lemon juice

1 tablespoon dried dill weed

1 tablespoon tomato paste, divided

½ teaspoon salt

⅛ teaspoon black pepper

24 yellow and red baby bell peppers

¼ cup vegetable, chicken or beef broth

1. Heat oil in medium skillet over medium heat. Add onion and cook until translucent, stirring occasionally.

2. Add ground beef and cook 6 to 8 minutes or until browned, stirring to break up meat. Drain fat. Transfer meat to large bowl. Add rice, parsley, lemon juice, dill, 1½ teaspoons tomato paste, salt and black pepper. Mix until well combined. Set aside.

3. Cut small slit in side of each baby bell pepper and run under cold water to wash out seeds. Fill each bell pepper with 2 to 3 teaspoons seasoned beef. Place bell peppers in **CROCK-POT**® slow cooker, slit side up. Add broth and remaining 1½ teaspoons tomato paste. Cover; cook on **LOW 5 hours** or on **HIGH 2½ hours.**

makes 16 to 18 servings

Bacon-Wrapped Fingerling Potatoes with Thyme

1 **pound fingerling potatoes**

2 **tablespoons olive oil**

1 **tablespoon minced fresh thyme**

½ **teaspoon black pepper**

¼ **teaspoon paprika**

½ **pound bacon**

¼ **cup chicken broth**

1. Toss potatoes with oil, thyme, pepper and paprika in large bowl.

2. Cut each bacon slice in half lengthwise; wrap half slice bacon tightly around each potato.

3. Heat large skillet over medium heat; add potatoes. Reduce heat to medium-low; cook until lightly browned and bacon has tightened around potatoes.

4. Place potatoes in **CROCK-POT®** slow cooker. Add broth. Cover; cook on **HIGH 3 hours.**

makes 4 to 6 servings

Tip: This appetizer can be made even more eye-catching with rare varieties of potatoes. Many interesting types of small potatoes can be found at farmers' markets. Purple potatoes, about the size of fingerling potatoes, can add some more color and spunk to this dish.

Asian Chicken Fondue

2 cups chicken broth

1 cup shiitake mushrooms, stems removed

1 leek, chopped

1 head baby bok choy, coarsely chopped

2 tablespoons oyster sauce

1 tablespoon mirin

1 tablespoon teriyaki sauce

2 pounds boneless, skinless chicken breasts, cut into 1-inch cubes
Salt and black pepper

1 tablespoon canola oil

1 cup seeded and cubed butternut squash

2 tablespoons cold water

1 tablespoon cornstarch

1 can (8 ounces) baby corn, drained

1 can (8 ounces) water chestnuts, drained

1. Combine broth, mushrooms, leek, bok choy, oyster sauce, mirin and teriyaki sauce in **CROCK-POT**® slow cooker. Cover; cook on **LOW** while following remaining instructions.

2. Season chicken with salt and pepper. Heat oil in large skillet over medium-high heat. Add chicken; cook and stir about 8 minutes or until lightly browned. Stir into **CROCK-POT**® slow cooker. Stir in butternut squash. Cover; cook on **LOW 4 to 4½ hours.**

3. Stir water into cornstarch in small bowl until smooth. Stir baby corn and water chestnuts into **CROCK-POT**® slow cooker. Whisk in cornstarch mixture. Cover; cook on **LOW 20 to 30 minutes.**

4. Serve with bamboo skewers, fondue forks or tongs. Broth may also be served in small soup bowls.

makes 6 to 8 servings

Channa Chat (Indian-Spiced Snack Mix)

2 teaspoons canola oil

1 medium onion, finely chopped, divided

2 cloves garlic, minced

2 cans (15 ounces each) chickpeas, rinsed and drained

¼ cup vegetable broth or water

2 teaspoons tomato paste

¼ teaspoon ground cinnamon

¼ teaspoon ground cumin

¼ teaspoon black pepper

1 bay leaf

½ cup balsamic vinegar

1 tablespoon brown sugar

1 plum tomato, chopped

½ jalapeño pepper, stemmed and minced, or ¼ teaspoon ground red pepper (optional)*

½ cup crisp rice cereal

3 tablespoons chopped fresh cilantro (optional)

Jalapeño peppers can sting and irritate the skin, so wear rubber gloves when handling peppers and do not touch eyes.

1. Heat oil in small skillet over medium-high heat. Add half of onion and garlic. Reduce heat to medium and cook 2 minutes or until soft. Transfer to **CROCK-POT®** slow cooker. Stir in chickpeas, broth, tomato paste, cinnamon, cumin, black pepper and bay leaf. Mix well. Cover; cook on **LOW 6 hours** or on **HIGH 3 hours.**

2. Meanwhile, cook balsamic vinegar and brown sugar together in small saucepan over medium-low heat. Cook until vinegar is reduced by half and mixture becomes syrupy. Set aside.

3. When chickpeas are cooked, remove with slotted spoon and place in wide bowl. Allow to cool 15 minutes. Toss with tomato, remaining half of onion and jalapeño pepper, if desired. Gently fold in crisp rice cereal and drizzle with balsamic syrup. Garnish with cilantro.

makes 6 to 8 servings